Raised By Wolves:

a Memoir

The semi-true stories of the early days in
poetry, remembrances, and illustrations by

Bill Comeau

Including: Some Later Reflections

Sugarhouse Press

Freetown, Massachusetts

"Putting local pen to global paper"

www.sugarhousepress.com

Published in the United States by Sugarhouse Press. Distributed by www.lulu.com.

ISBN #: 978-0-557-49138-4

Prologue

This is a collection of poems and recollections based on stories I remember or heard growing up in the small city of Haverhill, Massachusetts and the small towns of Danville and Hampstead, New Hampshire. They reflect my favorite story tellers: James Thurber from whom I learned the art of simple illustrations to help move the story along; Jean Shepherd who told me stories on the radio when I was supposed to be asleep in my bedroom; and Garrison Keillor, my Saturday Night "Lake Wobegon" radio fix; and Don Bliss, a member of our radio show cast - the "Gloryland Parson Band".

The Gloryland Parson Band

Bill   *Don*   *Dave*   *"Davis"*

D-day Remembers

Church bells
In the middle of the day.
D-day
And those who could not fight
Marched in the streets.

A rag-tag band.
Out-of-tune troubadours,
Honking and squeaking,
Clanging on pots and
Beating the drums.

I marched
At the head of the parade.
Small flag waving in small hand.

I smiled and walked tall
(as tall as any six-year old can stand)
In front of the band.

I did not understand
Until much, much later
That somewhere the sand ran red.
The dead and dying
Providing the "D" for D-day.

"The poem that inspired the cover art."

Also by Bill Comeau:

Voices from September 11th
(with Don Bliss)

Greetings From Comeauville:
100 Short Poems, 1955-2010

The Wit and Wisdom of Willy the Dog

and more...

All available from Sugarhouse Press

Introduction

by Lee Allen Hill

Alas, I was not raised by wolves but by Republicans. Oh, they did their best, but to them the moon hung too high to inspire a second glance, much less a song.

I met my first wolf, Bill, when I was thirteen. He came shambling into New Britain, Connecticut with a pretty young wife, and the beginnings of a family all packed up in a Gibson hard-shell guitar case. There was plenty of room in there, because the guitar, an aptly-named Hummingbird, never seemed to lie down. Nor Bill, either, as far as that goes.

Everyone knows wolves crave the community of the pack (kids now call them posses, and probably will for the next twenty minutes). Even in New Britain, Bill had little trouble attracting a throng of like-minded and moonstruck fellow travelers. It has always been that way with Bill. There is always a pack. But whether it is he who finds us, or we who find him I am unable to determine. All I know is that in our 45 years of mutual---if patchy---history, I have never known him to be without the company of the most talented, most creative creatures his current neck of the woods has to offer.

The mid-60's finds New Britain, the soon-to-be former "Hardware Capital of the World", a wrecking-ball wreck of so-called urban renewal and complacent, blinder-ed denial. Meanwhile its First Congo Church---the country club church---stares equally blindly into the oncoming light of a freight train of social revolution. Then here comes Bill with a bagful of protest songs, and a bellyful of belly laughs, and a spiritful of bo-doh-dee-oh bo-doh-dee-oh-doh. To the old and self-satisfied in the church he is 'gasp!' To the young and searching he is 'aha!'

At thirteen-years-old, my rightful piece of the Bill pie was JPF (Junior Pilgrim Fellowship, yeah really, huh?). But due to circumstances I've never quite understood I was allowed to double dip in SPF. On some occasions I was even invited to participate with the Young Adults. I remember a particular Young Adults weekend retreat I was invited to attend. Bill let me help him shoot a movie (tres artsy), introduced me to Lynn, a self-proclaimed black

Scotsman in a tartan cap, and taught me to play the confounding game of Kashultz (where something means nothing and everything means the same). I was just a pup, of course, and kept pretty much to the fringes of the older society, but these were heady times, indeed, and shaped me and set the template for the society I will always seek.

In 1964 I thought Dylan was pronounced Die-lan, and wondered 'who was this Dillon guy everybody was talking about?'. In 1965 I bought a pawn shop guitar and began writing protest songs before I even learned to tune the blasted thing.

Bill's tenure in New Britain was too short, but long enough. He left behind a strong and vital pack that existed to one degree or another for many moons. Mark. Shea. The two Toms. Linda. Others who eventually drifted. And I, who did some drifting of my own.

I followed Bill figuratively for several years. Then, literally again in the mid-70's. He called me one day and said, "You still writing?" I was. "You think you could write ads?" I didn't know. "Sure you can." So I wrote ads and enjoyed the work as well as the society of a new pack, in a different wood.

Eventually I followed Bill from Farmington, Connecticut to Providence, Rhode Island. Everywhere a pack gathered. The talented. The inspired. The searching.

Bill says he stayed in advertising too long. Maybe I did too.

When I recently reconnected with Bill and learned that he was assembling these stories and remembrances, I was prepared to pester him for a preview. "Sure," he said. "Where shall I send them?" Such trust and generosity. How could I have doubted it?

I read these stories, many of which I'd already heard in the oral tradition, with a vague sense of propriety. While they are not my stories, they make me somehow homesick, like a familiar but long-lost scent on an evening breeze. Or the shadows of ancestral remembrance and yearning created by a bright and baleful moon.

Then Bill asked me to write this introduction. And I went bo-doh-de-oh, bo-doh-de-oh-doh.

Lee Allen Hill   ---   January, 2010
AKA Lee-The-Pup, JPF, SPF, Young Adults   ---   1965

Chapter One
Fortified With Vitamin "P"

Being the first child in the family, an only child, and <u>the</u> only grandchild for about ten years, every event in my life became a family celebration. Take changing time for example. It was the era of cloth and safety pins. I was the first kid on the block with a piercing. It's how I developed my earsplitting singing style, very useful in the coming rock and roll invasion. Well, one day the tag team designated to do the deed was mom and Nurse Narnie (a.k.a. Aunt Ethel).

Their timing was off and the diaper was dry, but the cool breezes sent a signal to my sprinkler system and the fountain of the youth streamed a perfect arc into a big bowl of potato chips next to me on the couch. I was just contained with cloth and pins when the three Comeau brothers came in from whatever current invention they were inventing. They found three semi-chilled Nasty-Gannsets in the icebox and were in search of a snack when dad spied the chips. Well, the old block grabbed 'em and began a munch fest. Nurse Narnie and mom got to snickering and refused the offer of the bowl of happiness. "Say," Uncle Al ventured, "these chips sure are salty, just the way I like 'em." "I'm sure they are," quipped Nurse Narnie, "and they're good for you." "How do you know that?" dad asked with a handful ready to be chomped. "Well," mom intoned in her proper New Hampshire accent," they are fortified with vitamin 'P'." After which she and Nurse Narnie were reduced to such laughter that they nearly dampened their drawers.

Playground Language 101

When the cops would leave,
all the big guys like
JoJo Saratore's big brother,
Aram the Armenian,
and Big Shindee
would start shooting craps again.

We would edge as close as we dare
And watch 'em "roll dem bones".
They played for real money,
We played for bottlecaps.

Every once in a while
We'd learn a new word.
(the kind that were scratched
Into the olive green paint
on the boy's room door).

Once Big Shindee
dropped a bundle
trying to make a pass the hard way
and
I learned five new words
Before the cops come back
And we all ran for home.

"They were worth a bar of Ivory in the mouth."

Chapter Two
Raised by Wolves

I think I was raised by wolves. They were loved ones who loved to bay at the moon. Whatever they did to put a roof over my head or bread on the table, music was really why they were alive. It all came clear to me when they built a barroom next to my bedroom. I don't mean that there was a bar next door to where we lived; it was the room next to my bedroom. You went from bunk beds and signed baseball cards to booths, neon signs, and a cool jukebox.

I was always welcome and had a sip of whatever was being served and was allowed to fill my young lungs with second-hand smoke. Of course, my favorite beverage was a Roy Rogers (no silly little girl Shirley Temple for me). It was ginger ale in a tall glass with a shot of cherry juice and about four or five healthy soggy cherries colored with the finest number 5 red dye. Yum!

I sat on my favorite barstool and listened to the Andrew Sisters telling their boyfriends: "Don't sit under the apple tree with anyone else but me." It was just after WWII and my uncles were just home from saving the world by stamping out evildoers. I guess they missed a few because we're still sending young men and women, our youngest and best, over there.

Toy Soldiers

Tin Generals

Lay among broken troops

In

Toy box

Old soldier's home.

Once

It was their barracks.

Once it was where

The Generals

Planned mighty battles

Among

Baseball cards and bottle caps.

Once upon a simpler time,

Before

The Commander-in chief

Grew up and went off to fight in

A grown-up war.

"Life story in a toy box"

Chapter Three
My Wolves Were Wonderful

My wolves were wonderful. I was the first kid in the family and nobody knew about rules. I can't remember any except not to miss a meal. If you could see photos of me at that time you could see that I never did. I'd head out the door quietly before the Hangover Club was up and run down to the LaPrell household. Mrs. LaPrell would be whistling up a storm and getting her husband and older kids off to work. She always set me a place at the table and ask, "Billy, how you want your eggs or fried?" Sounds good to me.

Then Ronny would come downstairs and I'd have cereal with him. Last would be Pokey who only wanted toast. I couldn't let him eat alone for crying downtown. Then we'd head to the playground to play… hence the name. About noon we'd go to my house for ham sandwiches and orange soda, which we called "tonic", then back to playing in the woods (six trees and a tiny brook).

About sundown my wolf stomach growl brought me back to the Laurel Avenue den. There was always the same plate prepared: boiled meat, a plethora of potatoes, and whatever canned vegetable was in season. Yum. I would wash it down with a healthy dose of more Orangeade. Double Yum! Dear God, I forgot the Bread and Butter. Let us not forget the omnipresent bread and butter. WonderBread that built bodies between 8 and 12 ways, depending on what the Ad Agency thought they could get away with that month and soft butter, left on the table all day to get it the way Bumpa liked it.

During the war it was lard with some horrible yellow coloring. Yuck. Fortified, I would head-off in search of other young wolves in search of fun and frolic until the Wolf Air Raid Siren would shatter the night air. It was Nana screaming, "Billy, BILL-Y, BillyComeHome!" For a while I thought my last name was *Comehome*.

Home was a cozy den where the family gathered around the old Philco radio and listened to hear when Fibber Magee was going to open that overstuffed closet. Every family had a junk closet, but the one on the Fibber Magee and Molly show was of Olympic class. After that we'd be glued to the set because at any time the Shadow was going to finally reveal "What Evil Lurked in the hearts of men (and women too, I guess)." Then maybe we could put an end to war forever.

The Woods

In the woods

There as a big tree

And somebody

(Bughouse Miller's older brother)

Tied a really thick rope

To a really high branch.

I think the rope was

Stolen

From the railroad yard.

Anyhow

The tree was

On the edge of the cliff

And you could swing

W a y t h e h e l l o u t

Over the little stream

And   let   go!

(God it was scary)

That's how you made your bones.

The difference between being

Chickensh*t

Or one of the gang

Was about

20 feet.

"If our parents ever knew."

Chapter Four
Nana to the Rescue

I spent every summer at the camp on Sunset Lake in Hampstead, New Hampshire. Bumpa and his boys had built it from recycled lumber he "salvaged" when the Boy Scouts tore down their campsite on Long Pond. It was called "Idle Hours" but Bumpa found so many tasks for Al, Art, and Joey to do that they tore down the sign and floated it off in the brook in the back yard. The shore was a mite rocky, so Bumpa talked a friend in the town into delivering several loads of beach sand to our waterfront. They "fell off the truck" as I heard it told and one load was set near the beach to become my personal "Imagination Land".

It was here that with a popsicle stick I laid out roads through Comeauville. I planted tiny trees and built sand camps and spent hours making Varooom noises as tiny cars and trucks traveled through the village. One year I asked the Claus Man for two Farm sets from the Sears Dream Book and my village was heavy into farming all summer long.

The other sand found its way to the water's edge and with rakes flying, Bumpa and the boys cleaned out the muck and made a nice swimming area. Later, the Sunset Lake Improvement Association took care of all the camps in our area. It was a wonderful place to play for me and my little pals. Nana would sit on one of the beach chairs that Bumps built reading her "penny dreadfuls" while we built castles with plastic pails full of sand.

I remember Nana getting very "into" her reading. At times she would laugh out loud. Other times she would turn a shade of crimson beneath her stylish sun hat and mutter,"Oh My, Oh My Goodness Grapes and Gravy." I never understood that reaction but I like the thought of Grapes and Gravy. At that age I loved the thought of Gravy over anything as it was served to "Cover a multitude of Kat'rin's cooking mistakes," the boys would mutter at the supper table being careful not to let Bumpa hear their complaints.

Well one beautiful Sunset Lake morning my pals and I were in a frenzy of castle construction in what we thought was the safest place on God's Green Earth until little Janet LaBlanc whispered to me, "Is that wiggly thing Grapes and Gravy?" It wasn't. It was a snake that had tired of tempting nubile Eves with forbidden fruit and came to pay us a visit in the sand box. I was transfixed at how it moved without legs when I noticed a "Penny Dreadful" flying through the air and Nana moving faster than I thought possible while evoking the entire Holy family in a single breath.

Where she found the "Oar of Death" I'll never know but within seconds what had been a single water snake was cut in twain and continued wiggling around the sand castles with one end hissing and poking out the forked tongue of Satan himself. Nana was screaming in a voice that would peal the bark off a tree and we were running towards the camp at full-tilt-boogie speed. Nana had summoned the strength of the Gods and proceeded to dice the offending critter into tiny modules of snakeness. "Get into the camp," she screamed at us, and by God we did.

Now gentle reader, in sharing this story with my shrink later we discussed issues of castration anxiety. I only know that to this day I hate snakes and have a fear of overbearing woman carrying oars.

If You See Me, Take Me Home

"O where have you been,
Billy Boy
Billy Boy?

O where have you been
Charming Billy?"

Someplace beyond
Where I started and
Completely
R e m o v e d
From where I thought
I was headed.

Please keep my dinner warm.
I do want to come home.

"Enjoy the journey, dear friends"

Chapter Five
Bughouse Miller and the
Left Overshoe Disaster

We played a game called "bike hockey" on the seldom used street by the Wood School playground. All we needed was an old boot (our preference was a used left overshoe I found in the cellar before Bumpa threw everything away) and a half dozen fools on old bicycles. The object was to kick the boot under old man Miller's rotting Chevy truck that was always parked on the street because it no longer worked, just like old man Miller.

You would tip your bike on its side and with your free leg; kick the boot with all your might hoping to get it past the other intrepid hockey bikers and under the truck. There was a great feeling when your Keds made solid contact and that old rubber boot with its rusty metal snaps was sent flying. Hacker Hall was pretty good but Ronnie "Scope" LaPrell was better. Pokey and me were terrible and Bughouse Miller was the worst.

His sister was sent home once by the head lice police and the name "Bughouse" Miller was born and unfortunately stuck, keeping him from running for Congress but not from the local police. His style was to tip his bike one way and kick with the opposite foot causing a series of amusing crashes and a stream of blue words he had learned from his older brothers who were in the Navy at the time.

One fine day in Haverhill, we were assembled for the Olympic tryouts (or so we told ourselves). In addition to the regulars there were the two Shindees (Big and Little) and a kid I only knew as CaCa. I was called CoCoa and never asked why he was called by such a brownish nickname, but you always wanted to keep upwind of him if possible. Now Big Shindee was definitely the crème de la crème of bike hockey-ists. He had to be, he was only five foot zero and weighed close to 300 flabby pounds. Bumpa said if he sat on a barstool at the Old Stein Tap he would have an automatic hangover. It took me a while to get that joke until I saw him on his antiquated Schwinn. When he rode away from you it looked like two kids fighting under a blanket.

Anyhow, when he got the full weight of his Big Shindee left foot on that Boot, it would take you off your bike if it hit you. So, as luck (mostly bad) would have it Big Shindee was Hell bent for the old overshoe from the north side of the Tucker Avenue and the intrepid Bughouse Miller was tearing up the tar from the south.

Bughouse got there first and swung the wrong foot with a ferocious grunt just before the collision.

There were bike parts flying everywhere and poor Bughouse might have met his Maker then and there except he landed on top of Big Shindee. They both slid over the hill into the middle of a pickup baseball game, scattering bats, balls, gloves and kids in all directions. I saw the famed left overshoe slide neatly under the Chevy. "Score," I yelled before laying down in the middle of the street along with Little Shindee, Hacker, Scope, Pokey and even CaCa to laugh our collective and individual asses off.

We howled and hooted with tears streaming down our faces as six ballplayers tried to put Big Shindee together again and Bughouse entertained the crowds with a cloud of new blue words fresh from his Navy brothers.

It was only later that we found the secret to the famous Bughouse kick. We found the pedal from Bughouse's bike safely ensconced in the toe of Bump's old left overshoe. Big Shindee never played bike hockey with us again and Bugs walked with a limp until 7th grade.

Playground Helper

In the summer,
The Haverhill Parks Department
Would hire college kids
To take us on trips
And
Teach us life skills,
Like gymp.

This one summer
We got this very pretty girl type
Who didn't look or smell
Like any of the local girls and
Everybody fell in love.

Hacker and Scope
Were downright silly
And Pokey and me just giggled.

Then JoJo Saratore's big brother
Got home from the Navy
And started
Hanging around
The playground and she didn't
Teach us no more.

Chapter Six
The Day that little Billy died.

I remember shaking my female dolls and gritting my teeth. My mother would grit her teeth when she was angry. She was angry a lot. I don't know why but I can guess. She didn't want to be married so young. She didn't want a kid so young. She had spent her girlhood raising her youngest brother after her mother died too young. Mom was ten and Rich was two and that was that.

Her dad was a cold Swamp Yankee. She had a duty to perform. So she did. Her grandmother helped, but there was no warmth in Nana Currier that I could remember. So when she fell in lust with her second musician, my dad, and was with child she escaped the frying pan and leaped into the fire. They had no money. She lost the prestige of being one of the better families in her small town and became a young woman with a younger husband, and soon an enfant terrible. So I shook my female dolls, I gritted my teeth; I put their heads under rocking chairs, and hid behind the couch when it came time for toilet training.

I was scared to death of my body falling apart so when asked if I had to go to the bathroom, I lied. I was so afraid of displeasing the one who shook me with that grimace on her face, I lied every chance I got. When she was happy with me, there were healing hugs and the warmth of her perfumed body engulfing me. But, when she abandoned the bad little Billy, I tasted Hell on earth. No one else knows this, but I think it was when little Billy died.

When others were around she smiled and patted me on the head and the gaggle of aunts and soon-to-be aunts worshipped me. I was the only child in the family. I became the Crown Prince of Comeauville. Anything I wanted magically appeared.

Dad was a mysterious figure who tried to work when he could and was asleep on the couch when he couldn't. He was always the "big threat". "Wait 'till your father comes home." He came home he asked me what happened, grunted, then headed for the couch. So I learned early that to control life, I simply had to tell them what they wanted to hear. It always worked and it is still working.

Gentle Reader: ponder with me this early training. Was I battered? Was I shaken until my freckles fell off? Was I conditioned that anything was better than being a bad little boy? Is that when Little Billy died? I think not. He lives in my skin and in my reflex conditioning. Perhaps that's why I am drawn to a God whose love is unconditional. Who knows and who will ever understand? Perhaps I will, someday.

To Eden with Hope

Why is it that
When truth confronts
The lusty prophetess of doom,
She runs into her secret room to pray?

What magic words will she recite?
To fend away the coming night and
Turn the darkness into day?

Whoever would while flames remain
To torment those without a name in Babylon,
Be fool enough to doubt her spell?
For when the final daylight dawns
Exposing all the broken pawns
To tarnished knights and polished kings,
To silver queens with ruby rings
Around their souls
Will call from Hell
To secret lovers they knew well in Babylon.
Each must obey Earth Mother's will
And yield up all to her,
Still the haunting memories will bring
Wild promises of Spring
To all who loved with Adam
In the Fall.

Ah, Mother Eve, return to spawn
A purer crop when we are gone.

Chapter Seven
Never Name Your Dinner

During the WWII years, you could tell what day it was by the meal that was on the table. Wednesday was Prince Pa'sketti Day and if the budget allowed one meatball each. Thursday was something called Welch Rarebit that had more to do with saltines and molten cheese like substance than long eared critters. Them Welchers musta been mighty poor hunters.

Friday was always fish of some kind 'cause the Pope said so. Saturday was beanies and weenies. The beans in a ceramic crock spent the day in the furnace and they had a slab of salt pork and molasses to make 'em extra yummy. I know I forgot Monday and Tuesday which were always "Pot Luck" or clean out the fridge days.

Then there was Sunday, Blessed Sunday. A chicken in the pot Sunday, with smashed white potatoes and stuffing and a boatload of gravy. Bumpa always ate the neck, the Pope's nose, and other innards too disgusting to name. We always had chicken.

We raised our own. They were for eggs and as I learned the hard way, for Sunday's feast. One of my jobs was to feed the chicks and to gather the eggs. It was fun. I could even tell some of them apart from the others. My favorite was a sweet little hen named Miss Feathers. We chattered about important stuff like eggs and feathers and how much I hated school and loved summer vacation. Now, before you think that I was akin to a fool, I had seen Bumps chasing headless chickens around the yard on Saturday afternoon, but he said they were stray chickens who had come into the yard and offered to be Sunday dinner.

I remember Nana dunking the hapless critters into boiling water and removing their feathers and removing Bumper's favorite parts so there would be room for stuffing. I even remember making the stuffing by putting my grubby little hands into a bowl of stale bread, cool milk, fresh eggs, and spices and mixing it up to beat the band.

One Sunday just before feast time, I was playing with Pokey LaPrell sitting in the old wagon, pretending it was a Spitfire and giving what-for to enemy planes, when Nana's sweet voice

shattered the neighbor's porch windows telling me to send Pokey home and wash up for dinner. On the way to the back door I had to pass by the chicken coop and stopped to say hello to Miss Feathers. She wasn't in the coop.

I puzzled that all the way to the sink to wash off the residue of the gunfight we'd had with the enemy fighters. I was still wondering when I took my favorite spot at the table. Then my feeble Comeau brain became like Sherlock Holmes and even without Dr. Watson, I identified the bird coming out of the oven as Miss Feathers. I quietly excused myself and went into my bedroom to cry and from that day forth have never named a potential Sunday dinner. I can't even pick out a lobster in a tank. I just tell the waiter to surprise me.

Wilderness Youth

Harvey and me
Was gonna build
Our own log cabin,
We was.

Out there,
Just beyond the North pasture
Where the white birch
Were as thick as thieves.

We was gonna thatch a roof
With leaves and branches
From the notched wall logs,
Cause we dinnit wanta waste a thing, we dinnit.

We worked all afternoon
In the hot July sun before the dream died.

Musta cut down two, three small trees.
Pa was pissed cause we dulled his best axe, we did.

Ma just smiled,
And gived us bread and jam.

"Hard work always gets rewarded."

Chapter Eight
Religion 101

As you may imagine, the wedding of a 11th generation land-rich Baptist to a Cat'lic musician whose family was just off the Blue Nose Ferry from Nova Scotia was not an ecumenical celebration. Dad was 19 and mom was 21 and I was on my way into this world when the Justice of the Peace tied the knot. Hey, it was the 30's and he had flirty blue eyes and she had been married briefly before to a bandleader. Her dad was in Republican politics when there still were good Republicans in politics and he got marriage number One annulled.

Still they couldn't get married in a Cat'lic church, and when it came time to get me "done" so I wouldn't float around in un-baptized territory forever, they took me to Sacred Heart in Bradford. The well-meaning young priest looked up "who's in and who ain't" in the latest communication directly from Rome and I was found in the unwanted category. He told Dad, "No Way!" and Dad told him what he could do with the holy water. That's when we became un-churched.

It was the same wolf-like reaction that got him expelled from high school when Mr. Freeman told him all Canucks were "dumber than dirt." I don't know why it bothered him, Bumpa John was always saying, " The French are too dumb to die." A well placed ink well and dad was no longer matriculating at Haverhill High. This may have lead to my problem with authority that haunts me to this day.

So when it came time for Dad's funeral (evidently he wasn't too dumb to die at 36) I was not at all prepared for the rituals that took place. In the first place the concept of God was unclear and somewhat suspicious to me. I had prayed for stuff and never got it. I mean Santa delivered the goods. I asked God to spare my Dad and there he was asleep among the flowers in the front room. Either God didn't get it or I was doing it wrong, or maybe both.

The pot should not say to the Potter, "You didn't make me." The pot shouldn't say to the Potter, "I know more than you."

–II Samuel.

Windmills Revisited

The self-appointed knight
In his slightly tarnished armor
Rode at a gallop into enemy territory.

But when he discovered:
His maiden was not
Nearly in as much distress,
As he had been told;
And all the dragons
Were taking a nap in the afternoon sun;
He changed into
His finest tunic.

Then, alone
Among the un-tilted windmills,
He shared some wine with
His best friend,
And sat in the shade
To quietly write
One more
Classic poem.

"Ah, the story of my life, n'est pas?"

Chapter Nine
On Death and Dying

A car hit my dog Terry when I was about seven. After that my game became pacing myself with slow moving vehicles going down Laurel Avenue, and at the last possible moment, running in front of them. It was a life and death challenge that I always won. One October day however, it was raining and the street was covered with leafs. I challenged a slow moving Studebaker and right in front of it lost my footing. The driver slammed on his brakes and stopped inches from my sprawled body. Maybe. Maybe not. Perhaps I died that day and began part two of this dream dance.

Nana told me about her brother Danny that day. He was running to catch up with the wagon his dad was driving when he slipped. Just like me. His dad couldn't stop the wagon before the rear wheel crushed the right side of his head. They put a cloth over that side of his face at the wake. His mother didn't make up his bed for a week. The impression of his sweet face was still in the feather pillow. Now, all these years later, Nana still cries when somebody sings "Danny Boy". Thank God Mr. Studebaker had good reactions. I never raced another car.

When I was ten, the love of my life was Aunt Ethel (Narnie). She always had money to buy me what mom and dad couldn't afford. Her husband was a very successful bookie, but when he made the promises in front of the priest he must have had his fingers crossed. "Always running around with Floozies," Nana used to mutter under her breath. Floozies must have been bad cause they broke Narnie's heart. She found solace in cheap wine. It made her breath smell sickening sweet.

One night when we were dancing to one of the big bands on the Philco radio, she gave me a spin turn. I tripped over her cat and fell on her wineglass. It was a jelly jar; really, we couldn't afford wineglasses like they had in the movies. It broke and cut the middle of my right hand. I still have the scar to remind me of her.

I was too young to visit her in the Hale Hospital but I could stand in the parking lot with mom and watch her wave from the third floor window. The wine took her. She left me like Terry. I was ten and she was 33. Death and Dying.

Five years later, Dad was in the same hospital. He was there a lot. His heart wasn't up to code and the doctors said don't smoke and give up playing the saxophone. He cut back to three packs of Camels a day and only played four nights a week. For some reason fifteen was allowed to visit, so on Sunday mom and I ventured all the way from Bradford to Haverhill.

He was in a 50's-style oxygen tent. "You look funny in that thing," was all I could manage. "Well, I've been sick," he mocked and drew his cheeks in like the actor who looked like death warmed over on the Gleason show. I laughed. He could always make me laugh.

The next day, I was at the playground. We were all going on a trip to Canobie Lake Park. There was me and Hacker and Pokey, and Bughouse Miller and both Shindies (big and little). I was sitting on the home team bench with Hacker Hall talking about all the rides we would ride, when Ronnie LaPrell came toolin' up like the Devil hisself was on his tail.

"Nana says 'Go home'" he yelled to me, then spun around, kicked up dirt by third base and was gone. "Don't sound good," said Hacker. I jumped on my trusty, rusty Schwinn and took off after him. As I rounded the corner by Tavitian's Cash Market, the youngest Tavitian kid was yelling, "Ha, Ha, your daddy's dead."
His mother grabbed him and took him into the house as I banked the corner by Albert Bassani's hedge and within minutes skidded into the driveway at 54 Laurel.

Everybody was outside. There were tears everywhere. My cousin T.J. who was about four was asking what was getting into everybody's eyes. That's how it started. Everybody hugged me. We weren't a huggy family. Nobody said anything to me. They didn't have to, I knew. His odds had run out. When he was singing "Body and Soul" at the club on Saturday night, nobody knew it would be his last solo. It had been.

The front room was full of flowers. Dad was in a box against the wall where my bed would be after all was said and done. Grown men were bawling like babies. When it came time for the Rosary, Father Somebody got them all on their knees and Mom and I, the only non-Catholics, would take to the cellar until it was done. She sat in Bumpa's ratty barber chair and I held her hand.

Later at Sacred Heart there were bells, and smells, and Latin, and everybody crying. Nana was a wreck. Bumpa told me later as we built screens for the house windows, " A man should never outlive his kids." It was hot. It was July. It was my fifteenth birthday. Death and Dying.

It was fifteen years later. I was pushing mom's wheelchair down the corridor for another Chemo treatment. It didn't work. Too many packs of Marlboros for too many years. I stood by her bed. "I don't want to die," she whispered. I held her hand. She died, as I stood by helpless against the powers of death and dying. Death and Dying ruled the day.

My Father Art in Heaven

My father Art, who is in Heaven
(or at least deserves to be)
Was the leader of a small town band.

He would croon and smile at all the ladies
(mostly those never smiled at by singers)
So between sets he would
Hide in the kitchen with the crazy Chinese cook
(lest the smiles turn into something more).

Artie with the golden tenor sax,
Flirty blue eyes,
And deep, deep dimples.

When he died, the front room
Was filled with a sea of flowers, weeping men,
and a string of prayers.

I did not believe that any God
worth praying to could be so cruel,
so I hid from the overpowering
smell of the flowers
and the hollowness of the prayers.

My Mother, Dot, who is in heaven now,
Shares Art's smile once more.
Let it be so.

She smiles back
Beneath the flashing heavenly
Neon Narragansett sign,
And knows that all his smiles
For all the ladies dancing on the clouds
Are as they always were,
Only for her.

Sweet God, please!

"We all have a right to invent our personal view of heaven."

Chapter Ten
Aunt Hazel & the Stepped-on Cat

Bumpa John was from a large family, most of whom were listed in "Who's Who" under "What's This?" One of my favorites was Aunt Hazel. She was short, thin, and had the famous Comeau nose, the kind that can open beer cans if you are without an opener. She also had a voice like a stepped-on cat. She had a part-time job as the air-raid siren for Haverhill's shoe district and a laugh like very old pop corn popping in a sandpaper pan.

So, whenever I walked home from High School which really was uphill both ways, and I saw the beak and heard the demented cackle, I would do a dumpster dive lest she call my name at the top of her very large lungs. It wasn't that I was embarrassed but I was embarrassed. For one thing she never could say my name correctly, nor my Dad's for that matter.

We were both legally named Arthur. She like Bumper never met a "th" that she could pronounce so we became Arse-a. Not bad enough you say to dive a dumpster? Well add this: He was Big Arse-a and I was little Arse-a. If my high school buddies or the lovely and talented Janie Staples ever heard her call me Arse-a, I would've automatically sported a pocket protector, bought a slide-rule and joined the local chapter of Nerdonians United.

Then there was her habit of calling on us at home. You could hear the cackle approaching from Albert Bassani's house and, with luck, find a place to hide in time. Sometimes the cackle was missing and the first warning was that sweet foghorn voice yelling at glass shattering volume, "Any Body's ta Home, You?"

She never rang the doorbell, something about electric getting her and driving her crazy. As if! So Nana, all four-foot nothing of her, took a running start and leaped over the back of Bump's sleeping couch. I couldn't have been more surprised if I saw a miniature sled and eight tiny rain-critters.

I was so taken a-back that I fell in the middle of Nana's prized hooked rug laughing like I was watching a three Stooges Saturday matinee. I looked up to see that nose and a giant hairy eyeball pressed to the window and the air was split by "Little Arse-a, there you are. Come open the door you, for Auntie Hazel her." From behind the couch I heard, "Oh Brown Word."

My White Mountains

In my mountains
The Sun is captured
In diamond cages,
Released to
Rush over limestone boulders
And settle in the quiet valley
In my mountains
All the wild ones know
How to scurry away
From the crackling
Footsteps of
Heavy hunters.

In my mountains
There is
The promise
Of
Ultimate freedom,
If you know where
To look.

"When I asked Dad who made the
Old Man in the Mountain, he told me
God and the Glaciers."

Chapter Eleven

Wanted: Shadow the Ice Cream Thief

WANTED ICE CREAM THIEF

There are many Shadow stories. There's the time he and Bumpa John cut the next door neighbor's new boat in half; the time he ate a cake of Ivory and had Narnie and Mom running down Laurel Avenue screaming, "Mad dog, help us"; and the continuing saga of Ice Cream cones being stolen.

That's the one I remember the best having witnessed the technique of the pilfering pup on several occasions. His modus operundi was to hide all 80 pounds of his black shaggy self in the bushes and wait for an unsuspecting kid to exit Tavitian's Cash Market with a 10 cent two-scooper. Then, before you could yell to the kid that danger was afoot, two giant black dog tootsies where on his chest and a pink tongue the size of Cincinnati, exhaling foul doggie breath would have slurped the cone clean.

The kid would then do his best tonsil test and Old man Tavitian would come crashing out the front door thinking a murder was in progress. I would pretend not to know Shadow and go around the block the long way while the sugar-crazed black beast would high-tail it for home base. Nana would get a call and I'd have to take more money down to put in the Shadow jar. Now, I guess you can figure out the mad dog episode, but the "Shadow and Bumpa cutting a boat in half takes some explanation.

It seems wherever Bumps went Shadow was his shadow, hence the name. Screen doors were only a momentary bother for the philandering pup, so when Bumpa decided to test the outboard motor the Comeau boys had fixed one Saturday morning, he fixed himself his third hot water and Four Roses drink (Just a Toddy for the Body, Billy) and staggered towards the dock.

He had just untied the Billy-C and was ready to tug the starter rope when the Shads discovered that he had been abandoned in the camp. He backed into the kitchen and in two-tree bounds tore a Shadow-sized hole in the recently repaired (theoretically Shadow-proof) screen door. Another two-tree jumps and Bumpa looked up to see a Shadow blocking the sun.

For some reason the boys HAD fixed the motor and Bumpa's tug set the Billy-C in full motion just as Shadow landed on him. So as they say in my house, Da Bot of Dem hit the deck, Bumpa under 80 pounds of wiggly black fur. The boat never went as fast as it did that morning. The boys couldn't fix the motor so they had traded it for a more powerful new one. There they went ass over tea kettle, as Nana would say right for the middle of Mr. Dempsy's brand new, never been used, speedboat.

Those who viewed the crash (and the number of eye-witnesses grew with each telling) said Bumpa invented several new words (half French/half English) to describe the mutt licking his face as the Dempsy's "pride" and "joy" split ("pride" on one side, "joy" on the other) and sank with much gurgling and sputtering

It had been cut in twain by the now famous team of Bumpa and the Shadow.

"Dessum Cry Shadow what you do now?"

Chapter Twelve
Shadow Strikes Again

Of all the Shadow stories, my favorite was one I heard at Dad's wake. It seems that Aunt Julia's second husband couldn't take it any more. However, instead of just going out for a pack of Camels and never coming back, like husband number one, he choose to end it all in his summer cottage.

After a few "belts", Uncle Morris felt the urge to drain the doggie. And, speaking of doggies, because Shadow was such a pain in the posterior, Bumpa John had locked him in the upstairs bedroom that was next to the upstairs John. It was another example of Bumpa construction and the walls were thin and pliable.

Well Sir, Uncle Morris, bless his heart and less than adequate brain, managed to find the porcelain palace, however, the zipper on his "Sunday go to meeting" pants suddenly took on the characteristics of a Chinese puzzle. Even the muttering of the whole Holy family didn't help so he as they say at the shoe factory, "dropped trow".

I never knew if the deceased was Catholic or not, but all the family was and this was bad juju of the highest order. Nana and Bumpa had the biggest house at the time and so the wake took place in the front room. Uncle George was in a closed box from Murphy's Fine Funeral Parlor, and for most of the mourners became a talisman of fear. If you got too close would the accumulated guilt spill out and seep inside your soul like demons in the time of Jesus? One couldn't be too careful. One needed to muster all the courage one had to get close to the box, on your knees, while Father O'Somebody intoned what Bumpa called the Rosey.

Now Bumpa's youngest Brother Morris shared two things with Bumpa: the famous Comeau nose, and a metric boatload of superstitions. Add the circumstances of suicide and whenever the Rosey was chanted, they headed for the cellar where a quart of Four Roses, helped settle their nerves. Which after several hits caused Uncle Morris to need to drain his doogie.

Shadow was sleeping but hearing Uncle Morris creating a sound like a racehorse, he thinks it's his Masters stream and wants to be with him. He backs up to the bed and charges the wall and begins scratching it with his famous clown sized feet and let's out a howl that would wake the dead. This, needless to say, gets Uncle Morris's full attention in a stopped heartbeat. And that is why, gentle reader just as Father O'Malley gets to an Our Father, Uncle Morris, with Mr. Wiggly swaying in the breeze appears in the door way shouting, "Mon Gar, the Sumabitch is Alive Him!"

Boy's Pond

We used to swim naked
In Boy's Pond
And
Heaven help the girls
Who came to spy on us
(Heaven never had to help)

We used to dry off
In the back pasture
And
If the spirit moved ride
The cows into the noonday sun
Like
Little naked cowboys.

Sometimes
We would talk about
All the sex we'd have,
If and when we learned
What sex
Was all about.
(Heaven help us all.)

SILKY

When we were in
Seventh grade,
They brought into our school
A bunch of kids
From downtown
Cause their school had a fire.

One girl
Was Beverly Billadeaux
And Lennie and Charlie
And me was all in love.

We used to write her
Bad poetry and sign it
"From Silky."

Lennie moved to Ohio,
I lost track of Charlie
And by the time
We got to Haverhill High,
Beverly was all grown up
And
Hanging out
With the Greasers.

"First Love is a tough gig, n'est pas?"

Chapter Thirteen
Confrontation at the Lake

Bumpa had built a make-shift bridge across the little brook that ran behind the Camp into Sunset Lake. Nothing great. A Bumpa special. Couple of two-bys with scraps of wood nailed to 'em. Some of the nails were bent over because Bumpa's carpenter skills diminish in a direct relationship to the number of Toddies for the Body that he consumes during the project. There was no rail, so if you were a bit unsteady you would visit the turtles in the brook.

Like every Saturday night when Bumps came back from playing "penny ante poker" with Gertie, Bennie, et al, I would wait to hear that high tenor voice singing "I had a dream dear, you had one too." Then I would count to ten. About seven there would be a splash and the Lord would be summoned. Now, Gentle Reader, I thought the Lord's name was "Jessum Cry" until I was older. But, there would be a splash, Bumpa would be baptized in the brook and I would giggle. Another Saturday night at Sunset Lake.

Gayle moved in the summer of '52 and every red-blooded boy fell in love. I thanked Bumpa and the Lord for that silly bridge. It was a short-cut to Gayle's place. It was the summer following a three day a week work-out in Mike McGarr's basement with weights and springs. I was El Buffo, making up in defined muscle what I lacked in height. I was tired of being pushed around by Spats and his bully buddies at Haverhill High.

So, every day I would take my buff little bod over the Bumpa Memorial Bridge and Gayle and her fan club would soak up some rays. It didn't matter that her beach was rocky. We would talk about important summer stuff, listen to tunes, and every so often cool off in the spring-filled, cool blue waters of Sunset Lake. My view of Heaven, especially when Gayle dropped her towel and stretched before diving in.

That's when I heard a strangled, "Oh My God" coming from the road behind us. The sun was behind the speaker, and he looked like a villain in a Spaghetti Western. He looked ten feet tall. He wasn't. He was the kid who had followed us to Gayle's place from Mrs. Ellis's homemade ice cream emporium last week.

It seems he was nursing a crush the size of Kansas and the view of his intended beloved in a polka dot bikini had did him in.

What happened next was right of the back page ads for old Charlie Atlas. You know the one. There is some sand kicked and the runt of the litter skulks away while Brutus gets the girl. However, Brutus wasn't up to kicking stones, and I had finished my version of the Atlas course in Mike McGarr's cellar training facility.

There was strutting and posturing galore (Posturing Galore later became an exotic dancer, but that's another book). Gayle in the meantime, shrugged and dove into the lake.

Brutus had mistaken me for her boyfriend instead of a boy who was just a friend. So, I was the gatekeeper to the treasure in polka dots and needed to be vanquished. I stood up, flexing and doing some strutting myself. After all, never underestimate the power of teen age testosterone. Brutus started pushing me around more than somewhat. Gayle, meantime just giggled and swam out to the raft.

I pulled my 5' 4" frame to its most menacing height and tried to look tough. It failed. About that time Brutus' Dad arrived in an old Chevy rattle-trap pick-up truck. He was about to throw a leash on his semi-bright, pit-bull son when Brutus lurched at me. He was all arms and legs with very little in the brain department. I simply saw him as a bar-bell to be lifted, planted my feet and "clean and jerked" the jerk. Now with him over my head, I lowered his head a bit and did an imitation of the famous "Gorgeous George air plane spin" and walked out from under him. Brutus bit the dirt, rather the stones and lay there very confused. His Dad came over, thanked me for teaching his son a lesson and shook him awake. I was more than a little embarrassed so I ran towards the Bumpa bridge not knowing how to react to two Brutii. It must have been God who placed the broken Nastygannset bottle at just the right angle to put a major league cut between my great toe and the next in line. I hit the ground like a sack of rocks and was bleeding up a storm.

That's when I saw the Brutii heading towards me. "I'm done in." I thought to myself, but they picked me up, wrapped my towel around the offending foot and Chevyed me to Dr. Moore's office. Dr. Moore was everybody's doctor in town and put in a couple of stitches and bandaged me up. "No swimming 'till it heals" the good Doctor said. Brutus Junior shook my hand and they drove me back to the Camp where Nana invoked the whole holy family. I didn't see Gayle for a week and we never talked about the day I "clean & jerked" the jerk 'cause he really wasn't a jerk after all.

Chapter Fourteen
Julius John James
"Jiggs" Zamierowski, Jr.

I first met Jiggs in the third grade. We was buddies from the start except we were polar opposites. See, he was "bright as a button," Nana said. I wasn't even in the sewing kit. Not that I was as stupid as I seemed, I just was lost in my own private world. (I still am for that matter). Jiggs was great at sports, I played right field. He was picked first, I was picked after Bughouse Miller's little sister. She could out hit me, but I was a boy for crying over spilt milk!

At Haverhill High School, before Dad died and I moved to Hampster High, Jiggs would not study until after the late movie and then he would ace all his classes. Me, well I was ahead of Bughouse Miller's sister but not by much. But we was pals, me and Jiggs and after mucho years when we were all grown up and had real jobs I got an invite to his wedding. I had already been married and divorced twice, but that's another book yet to be written.

Now, Jiggs a.k.a. Julius John James "Jiggs" Zamerowski Jr. was 40 and had avoided wedlock for many years. Consequently, he had all the nickels he had ever earned and he had earned plenty. The lucky lady had the same number of names and was from Maine. So, I headed off to the adventure guided by a map supplied in the invitation. It took me from the Maine Pike to fairly well traveled secondary roads, down a dirt road, to a place to park the car and walk a slightly well-traveled foot path to a wooden structure overlooking the Atlantic.

There I saw the folks all gathered on the rocky beach and joined them in time to hear muffled voices making promises over the ever present Maine wind. It was beautiful and all, but with all the names on the invite, I had expected a Mansion instead of a Monsoon. After the ceremony we all climbed up the steep incline to the little wooden building for finger sandwiches and home brew. It was definitely my style of wedding.

Coming from the tiny kitchen was the smell of baking cake. I never met a cake I didn't like so I was pleased more than somewhat at the potential of sweet frosting et al. In the meantime I had discovered from a mutual friend that Jiggs and his bride had met skiing in Switzerland. Either he had saved her or she had saved him. So the intrepid Julia Child look-alikes were crafting a cake in the shape of the mountain range where love had nipped their frozen noses as it were.

The cake came out steaming and garnished by melting white frosting. There was no formality. Jiggs grabbed a hunk and fed his bride and she smushed a frosting blob in his face, much the amusement of all present. Now I tell you this story in order to thank Jiggs for the perfect opportunity for using the worst pun of my Olympic class pun career. When the room grew silent I said in my finest preacher voice, "Dearly Beloved, what we have here is a perfect illustration of the time-worn truth: If you want cake, The Lord Alps those who Alp themselves."

It Really is Falling

Now don't get nervous…or anything

BUT

Remember what Henny Penny told us

About the sky?

Well, it is.

"Ashes, ashes, we all fall down."

Chapter Fifteen
Dad Tries To Enlist

Uncle Joey and Al were both in the army so Dad wanted to join them. The problem was, he had a bad ticker from childhood ailments. That didn't stop him from trying. He stood in line for every branch of the service in his BVD's. He passed the eye-tests, the teeth counting; the flatfoot check and everything went well until the dreaded heart monitoring.

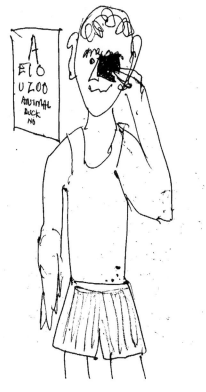

The Doc would give a listen; check to see if his stethoscope was working, and check one more time. Then calling on JesusMaryandJoseph he sit dad down and call a cab to take him home. He was worried that dad might expire right there on the government's nickel.

Well sir, one day between the ticker test and dad getting redressed, his cousin Scagy called him from the line just going into the eye test. "Art, I'm as color-blind as a blinking bat and I want to get into the Navy." "Not a problem," says Pops, and they exchange ID's. And that dear madam, sweet sir, is how a colorblind cousin got into the Signal Corps. (It is rumored that one day he told the Admiral to "Stuff It" from the deck of his ship).

Chapter Sixteen
Hunka Cole and his son Pick

D ad was famous for finding and befriending weird people. It's a trait I been blessed (or cursed) with as well. There was a semi-well known Captain of a charter Tuna boat out of Newburyport that latched on to dad in some bar he was playing. No surprise there. His given name was Jerome Cole but everybody knew him as Hunka. Every so often he would show up at our camp bringing a six-pack, a moth-eaten old Harmony guitar and his son named Pick.

After the proper number of libations were consumed he would launch into a colorful repertoire of bawdy ballads and questionable sea chanteys. He knew a few that would make a Baptist burn his bible. Nana would whisper about, "Little pitchers having big handles," meaning that I was sleeping in the main bedroom. "He's gotta learn sometime," Hunka drawled between sips of Nasty Gansett."

Dad would howl and Pick would giggle and Bumpa John would raise his head off the kitchen table and look as if Hitler was invading Sunset Lake. That not being the case, Bumps would let his head fall, bumping it on the table (hence the name) and slide back into his nightly stupor.

As it turned out not even Hunka's famous version of "Friggin' in the Riggin'," made it into my later solo career set list. It was Aunt Loraine version of "Coney Island Washboard Roundelay" that would become a signature song for the Incredible Broadside Brass Bed Band.

Every 4th of July she would sit on the back steps of the old camp and belt out several songs that never left me. She was an imposing woman who dressed in Muumuu's (think pup tent with arm holes) and with her official Don Ho Uke enchant the family with songs that included Hard Hearted Hannah throwing water on a drowning man, and her desire to shimmy like her sister Kate. The mental image of what was beneath that Muumuu shaking like jelly on a plate started earthquakes of hilarity to bubble through my youthful body.

Still it was the washboard making holes in a brand new pair of BVD's that made the set list and the Broadside's first and only album. If I hum a few bars, I can still see Washboard Mark, head thrown back and transformed into a whole new dimension of tranquility. Also there was the semi-famous version of my song "Little Dead Surfer Girl". I hope it's not all I am remembered for as a songwriter.

Dr. Demento used to give it and occasional spin. Several other insane bands also covered it over the years. The song reaches a fever pitch when Washboard gargles a plaintive echo to the lyric.

"Little Dead."
"Gargle-Gargle."
"Sir-fing."
"Gar-gle."
"Gir-er-erl." (Explosion of water sending the audience into flight mode.) Then there was the night the Smeltz switched Washboard's water with a glass of pure gin.

Chapter Seventeen
Paulie Battis Gets A Hit

I went to a very small high school. There were eleven in my class. Needless to say, I made both the basketball and baseball teams. Sometimes when it came time to play a game, we would have to drive around to kid's houses to scare up nine players.

That's how Paulie Battis, overalls, work boots, and his signature "eau de cow shit" aroma got to play against the Saugus Tigers that fateful fall day. Old Socco, our diminutive coach, who measured four foot nine with his elevator shoes and his hair slicked up tall with a pound of Brylcreem, put Paulie in right field which happened to be downwind that day. That moved me to center field. Well, Sir or Madam (as the case may be) the Tigers took the field in their new uniforms; they also had gloves and more than one bat for the team. Gasp!

The pitcher was about 23-years-old having stayed-back in every grade. I think the coach paid off the school board to keep him around, 'cause in the words of Old Socco, "Mother of God and all the Saints could that Sucker pitch." He was at least 6' 5" tall, lean as a string bean, and when he leaned back to throw the ball his hand touched second base.

It took all the courage I could muster, to stand up there with our one and only bat and listen to that ball whiz by like a pissed-off bee. Their catcher had stolen a couch pillow to put under his chest protector, and all his Mom's kitchen sponges to cram in his mitt. He still uttered a collection of brown words every time he caught the ball.

By some miracle we were only behind by one run in the ninth, the score being one to zip. That run was a homer that Goliath hit over the fence that is still orbiting Earth. Lucky we were playing at their place. We only had one ball, and that had tape holding it together. So when our best hitter, Pesky Comtois tore into a slow curve and got a double, we all cheered up a storm.

The we remembered it was Paulie's turn to bat. Old Socco called him over and whispered in his good ear (the one the cow didn't kick), I was standing right there, being up next. With two down in the last of the ninth, I was ready to go home, but I was up next. "Paulie", Coach said, "just bunt the ball and run like hell.

"O.K., Yup, I will". Quipped the wizard of right field, "What's a bunt?" Socco walked away patting his pompadour. So I moved close to Paulie and explained *sotto vocce*, "Just hold out the bat and let the ball hit it, then run like you do when your Dad has had too many Nasty Gansetts." "Oh yeah," Paulie responded, "I can do that… should I run for the woods?".

"No, just run down to First, O.K.?"

"Yup, O.K., I can do that," said the lamb ready for slaughter.

Well sir, the first pitch went by so fast Paulie never saw it. Neither did their catcher who caught it in the couch pillow and let out a "Woof" they could hear in Kansas. Pesky used the confusion to steal third and was now only 90 feet from our first tie game of the season. He did his famous "Ya Ya" dance that was designed to piss off the Pope. The pitcher turned a slow red. Nobody ever got to third on his watch. Nobody had scored on him since seventh grade.

I was so busy watching Pesky juking and jiving down the line; I didn't look at Paulie until it was much too late to yell at him. Paulie was so busy trying to remember three things at once that he had short-circuited his feeble brain tank. He had straddled home plate, closed his eyes and was muttering, "Run like when Dad is pissed, run like when Dad is pissed."

The pitching monster was watching Pesky as well, and didn't turn to look at Paulie until he released the fastest pitch of the day. From then on the world was in slow-mo. Me yelling, "Pau-lie No"; the ball hurling towards Paulie at the speed of sin; the catcher and the umpire diving out of the way to avoid flying Paulie parts; and Pesky running for home as fast as his French-Canadian bow-legs could carry him.

Now the God that protests drunks and silly children was working overtime that day. The ball hit our one and only bat on the trademark shattering it to smithereens; the ball then slowed tremendously got Paulie between the eyes and cold-conked him for sure. Pesky touched home plate as Old Socco punched me on the arm and yelled, "Run for Paulie". I did. It was my first and only home run as the ball flew over the fence.

Best season we ever had and there was no noticeable change In Pauline's behavior or I.Q., though he did claim to be abducted by aliens in later life.

"Run for the flour bag."

Elderberry Wine

We
Collected berries
All one morning
Getting
Scratches and
All itchy from
Backyard bushes.

We
Squeezed them all
Through Nana's
Cheesecloth
Until our fingers
Were
Properly purple.

Then,
We waited and watched
Everyday
After school
For maybe two, three weeks
For a miracle
That never happened.

"Maybe we should have added water."

Chapter Eighteen
Pesky's Perfect Potato Ploy

It all started with Ralphie Kelly eating his lunch sitting next to Pesky on the bench. Lunch was a can of sardines and a couple of raw potatoes that Ralphie was peeling with his Boy Scout knife. Pesky was our catcher that day and as he watched the spud turn into a pure white spheroid, a light went off over his curly black hair. Next thing you know, Pesky pilfered Old Socco's rule book and hunkered down to read it like I never saw him read before. Pesky had an aversion to all reading material that didn't have more pictures than words.

I was swinging the new bat we got after Paulie broke our other bat getting *Louisville Slugger*ed in the Saugus game. I looked at Pesky who had the look of a cat with Canary on his breath. Next thing you know he's getting Ralphie's last raw spud and heading behind the backstop.

I didn't think anything more about it until late in the game. The opposing team had a man on third with two down and was looking to go ahead of us. The ball came in about as fast as Dean Howard could throw it. "Bawl tree" called Umpire Levesque in his best Nova Scotia accent. I saw Pesky come around the batter and threaten the runner who was way off third base (Umpire Levesque would have called it "tird" base which would have had Ralphie Kelly dissolving into jelly at first).

Then I witnessed something I had never seen before. Pesky let fly and the pure white spheroid sailed over David Duston's head at third. Pesky never made a throwing error. The runner looked at the third baseman running towards left field, he looked at Pesky, looked at his coach, then came running as if the hounds of hell were nipping at his heels.

Imagine his surprise when he met Pesky, ball in hand waiting at home plate. He was almost as perplexed as Davey picking up a dirty potato in left field. The umpire said, "Yer OUT!" and the game was over. I was scratching my head as the two coaches and the umpire were poring through the rule book. Just then, Pesky came by me laughing to himself. "Taint nothin' in that there book 'bout taters," he laughed.

In the Mood for a Limerick

One minute he's walking on air.

The next he can just stand and stare.

It's no mystery to me,

I'm just like him you see.

He's my favorite bi-Polar bear.

me on a good day.

Chapter Nineteen
Ralph and Pesky Play it Cool

Meanwhile back at good old Hampster High, dear Old Socco, when he wasn't trying to kill us on the baseball diamond, surrounded us with hundreds of sharp objects of destruction in Ye Olde Shoppe Class. It was hotter than the hinges of Hades in shop that day. Old Socco had been called over to see Mr. Greenleaf the principal. The inmates were running amok in the institution, a small outbuilding next to the 100 year-old Hamster High School main building.

Now to let you know about what we were learning, no matter what plans we were given, we ended up making an ashtray. None of us could follow plans and Old Socco was as good at instructions as he was at coaching so what was supposed to be a coffee table, or a bookcase became an ashtray. I was working on my latest ashtray when Ralph Kelly and Pesky went by me. "Worry about zero," Ralph said and gave we a wink.

Ralph got out of work for years by pretending to be the dimmest bulb on the porch. He had mastered the perfect, "I didn't do it" look and would pretend to be following the path of a fly sailing around the room whenever a teacher would try to talk to him. His Tonto was Pesky, whose quest in life was driving Socco to the edge of distraction, then pushing him over.

I remember when he and Ralphie put a whistle and smoke bomb under the hood of Socco's pristine '48 Buick connected to the starter. It made a noise like the end of the World. "Worry about Zero," shouted El Ralpho and his diminutive dunce as the threw open the hood and attacked every wire with a couple of Socco's new golf clubs. The noise stopped and they had turned the puke green Grampamobile into…you guessed it…an ash tray on wheels.

Of course, the day I'll remember 'till it comes time for me to try to lie myself past the Pearly Gates, is that hot day in shop when Ralphie and Pesky headed outside telling me to, "worry about zero". Those were the magic words that usually meant: "It's time to blow this popsicle stand." No sooner had the door closed behind the Giggle Brothers, then I saw a hole appear in the wall at eye level. I backed up causing Paulie Battis to turn his custom baseball bat into a long thin ash tray.

I pointed to the wall and Paulie and I saw another hole magically appear. "Must be a deranged Woodpecker," ventured Paulie. "Got to be careful of 'em or they'll drill a holt in your cranium-brain parts," he continued. I thought it was most-likely a flock of Giggle Brothers birds, but figured Paulie was confused enough. As the third hole manifested itself Paulie dove under a bench and made cat noises to confuse the bird and I sprung for the door.

There they were Ralphie with the electric drill and Pesky manning the extension chord, laughing like loons. "Hey, Billy-Bob," said Ralphie, "Getting too hot in shop, so we is adding some natural air-conditioning." "Yes you are, indeed you are," I stage whispered and kept walking past old Socco and Green boy, as they approached Ye Olde Shoppe on a dead run.

Chapter Twenty
Never Give a Kid a Knife

When you are the only kid in the family, you usually get what you want. I wanted a knife. I wanted to learn to whittle like Bumps, but I needed a pocket knife. "He'll cut off a finger," yelled Nana prone to exaggeration. "Kid's gotta learn someday," Bumpa retorted looking at his scarred fingers. Bumpa cut sample shoes for Stein and Sulkis Footwear, and his fingers showed it.

So I got a pocket knife, and we sat together on the back steps whistling and whittling the snot out of helpless hunks of weed we found in the woods behind Carl Page's house. "I'm gonna whittle a sword," I told Bumps. "Anything but another GD ashtray," he grunted in response. We were having a fine ole time until I cut my would-be sword in half. "First lesson in whittling is every so often you need a new twig," Bumpa informed me. So I went into the woods (really seven scraggy pine trees and a mess of picker bushes) and found the twig to end all twigs.

It looked like a slingshot without the sling. A little cut here, some bark removal there and I'd be ready in case Goliath and the Philistines attacked Sunset Lake. I settled in next to Bumps who was enjoying his third Toddy for the Body of the morning. I put down my prize stick and began to open new trusty pocket knife with imitation mother-of-pearl sides. The knife was half open when I pointed out the project to Bumps with my finger under the partially open blade which choose that moment to slam shut.

"Jessum Cry", exclaimed Bumpa just as Nana came out the screen door to see a fountain of blood from my damaged digit damaging my new white T-shirt. "JesusMaryandJoseph," were evoked again as Nana clutched where she imagined he heart to be with her left hand, covering her eyes with her right. "I told you he would cut off his finger," she squealed running for the omnipresent Iodine and a fist-full of band-aids. "Kid's gotta learn sometime." Bumpa whispered under his Four Roses tainted breath.

It seemed that blood and snakes were both of equal screaming value in Nana's world. The bleeding stopped and I was

Iodined and Band-aided, and the knife got put in a drawer for the rest of the summer. Nana didn't speak to Bumpa for two weeks. I don't think that was a punishment. I still have the scar.

There's one more episode in the "knife" saga that I should share with you . It happened a few years later. I was in the habit of having a friend stay with me at the camp and since it was the time when Mom and Dad owned a small store in Atkinson, NH, I invited a boy about my age to spend a week. I didn't know him well and I didn't understand that he wanted to stay with me to be near his cousin who lived near the camp.

All went well until the night of the Annual Sunset Lake Improvement Association Shindig. It was a small town carnival without the rides. Assorted games and foodstuffs of a rural flair. It was also a place for all the teens to hang in the pre-Mall era. I had graduated from a pocket knife to a genuine hunting knife with a custom made leather sheath. It was my Dad's idea. "He's got to learn someday," Dad told Nana who lit some candles and pretended it didn't happen.

So there we were at the Shindig and the boy whose nickname was "Balls" and his cousin "Evil One" asked me if they could borrow the precious hunting knife. I should have known better but that kind of common sense was years away. So I handed it over and off they went to the hot dog tent. I was hanging around at the turtle race booth. (I supplied the turtles at 50 cents each). One turtle seemed hell bent on escaping and won all the races. I didn't think about much except to wonder if Summer Gayle was coming to her camp this year when Balls tapped me on the shoulder.

"You are in big trouble kid," he whispered. "Why?" I wanted to know. It seemed like a reasonable inquiry at the time. "Well", Balls continued drooling as he spoke. "You know that girl whose shorts are so tight she looks like she's smuggling peaches?" I turned to see Gayle in her favorite shorts and a top that would make grown men drool like sheep dogs. "Yeh, don't mess with her, she's got a boyfriend that would just as soon break you in two as look at you." "Too late," laughed Balls. At that moment, Evil One handed me back my hunting knife covered in red goo.

"You didn't," I snapped. "Nope," he did Evil said pointing at Balls. "Worse thing is we dropped your sheath and it has your name on it." "Balls, " I said, either referring to Balls or the situation. Then I did the type of thing that all BiPolar kids are apt to do. I grabbed the knife, jumped on my bike and headed for the lake. I don't remember untying the Billy-C or rowing out to the deepest part of the lake. I do remember throwing my new hunting knife in the water before returning to the Shindig.

When I got there Balls was laughing his balls off and the Evil One was rolling on the ground near the turtle booth. "What's so damn funny?" I wanted to know. "You sure are a sap," Balls said. "Yup, Yup, Yup," the Evil one echoed. Then he got up and handed me the sheath just as Gayle and her new muscle man arrived. "What?" I yelled. "Iffen you'd cleaned off the katsup you'd still have a hunting knife." The evil twins gasped as they jumped on their bikes and rode off into the Sunset towards Sunset Lake. Gayle wanted to know what that was all about? I could only admit to her and you, gentle readers, that I have an "L" for LOSER, tattooed on my forehead.

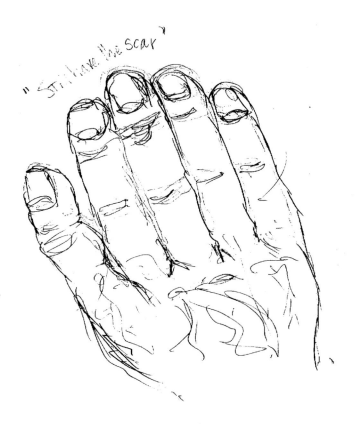

Note on God's Fridge

Dear One:

When you finish
C r e a t i n g
Whichever
U n i v e r s e
Is this week's project,
Don't forget
The bread and wine.

Luv ya !

"It could happen."

Chapter Twenty-One
Miss Hoyt and Hogg Corner

Miss Hoyt was older than God's eyebrows. She dressed in her best frocks from the Hoover administration, and smelled every so like moths without their balls. Plus she NEVER smiled.

At least no one still living could remember that look of her's. You know there's a look when you smell something bad? Miss Hoyt looked like she had just stepped in it.

She was also the self-appointed Guardian of Manners. So, every day when the lunch bell rang, she would position herself at the head of the escape stairs and each young person was oblarged to utter in a clear tone, "Excuse me, Miss Hoyt," as you squeezed past her enormous self. No, really, when she walked away from it was like two kids fighting under a blanket.

So one day just as I got to Miss Hoyt, Bugs Miller gave me an atomic wedgie, and while trying to extricate myself from yards of BVD's I neglected to kiss the Pope's ring, as it were. "Master Comeau," she sang out in a tone that froze the line from front to back. "Your problem is that since you live over to Hogg's Corner, you think you're too good to speak to us common folks from South Danville." "Am I right?" she continued.

I stammered like Elmer Fudd attacked by the Wraskely Wabbit, "No Miss Hoyt, your Madamship, I was accosted by an atomic wedgie and got distracted." "Young man, what on God's green earth is an atomic wedgie?" "Well," I ventured, "you know how if you wear your undies four days in a row, they sneak up in the crack of your sit-me-down?" She looked like she did when Ralph's pet snake got loose in History class. I was in too deep to stop now. "Well," I continued' "imagine how you'd feel if some son of a duck grabbed holt of 'em and yanked 'em up to your earlobes." She didn't move. She didn't smile. She simply retreated into the History room, closed the door and out-cackled Aunt Hazel.

Poverty Present

One day we sat on swings
At recess and
Talked about important
Fourth grade things.

Next morning
The snow covered the
Danville streets
And
His Dad never found
The way to our house
To pick up my Dad
To take him
To the Navy yard
Where they worked.

It had all gotten too much:
Money never enough;
Too many mouths to feed;
Work too damn hard;
And
Simple stuff
Toilet was broke, rent was due
Wife pregnant again.
What was a simple man to do?
So,
In the middle of the night
He decided
To give the whole family,
Death for Christmas.

Chapter Twenty-Two
Waterskiing Made Semi-Easy

We had seen pictures of people riding behind speed boats on water skis. They were mostly beautiful people in cigarette ads on the back covers of the Saturday Evening Post. However, there wasn't a boat on Sunset Lake that could pull skis. No one dared to purchase such a speedboat since Bumpa and Shadow had cut Mr. Dempsy's pride and joy in twain. I guess they were afraid to invest in such a boat while Bumpa and Shadow were still on the loose.

So, one Sunset Lake day, me and the Foley boys decided to reinvent the sport with the Billy-C, and a small pair of snow skis with rawhide laces we found in the shed. We figured that the souped-up, 2 and ½ rpm trolling motor would probably work. After all if it cut a boat in half, it could probably pull a small skier like me. I sat down on the side of the raft facing Tel Noah Camp and strapped on the skis.

It was swim time at Tel Noah and all the well-endowed young Jewish Girls were watching and giggling. There I was ten feet from shore and standing on the Foley's raft. Clyde "Clutch" Foley was manning the motor. Ducky Foley was on look-out, and Johnny was on the raft with me. "You sure the straps'll hold ya," inquired Johnny Boy. "Yup", I said, "I laced 'em real tight."

"OK, Clutch, Let her rip," I yelled. Clyde the Glide let her rip. The rope played out behind the Billy-C, and I felt myself moving towards the end of raft. "You need a push," Johnny yelled and supplied one. The Billy-C pulled away at a blinding 2 MPH and I hit the water with an impressive splash. The last thing I remember is a ripple of teenage girl laughter as my wooden skis made their way to the surface. I glanced around at several confused sunfish, a terrified hornpout and a skittish pickerel.

I had nixed the idea of tying the tow rope around my waist (God looking after fools like me) so all I had to do was get out of the rawhide straps which, as you my know shrink when wet. So I let go of the tow rope and "swam" towards the multicolored bikini bottoms at the Tel Noah beach club. I give blessings to the lifeguard type and the gaggle of beauties that dragged me to the shallow water.

I came to the surface surrounded by giggling rescuers and looked like Mosey the cat when he fell in the brook trying to catch a sunfish. I had planned to look like the cool dudes in the cigarette ads. So much for those plans, and the plans to be the first to water ski on Sunset Lake. I did meet a wonderful girl from Brooklyn named Naomi, however, so the day wasn't a total loss.

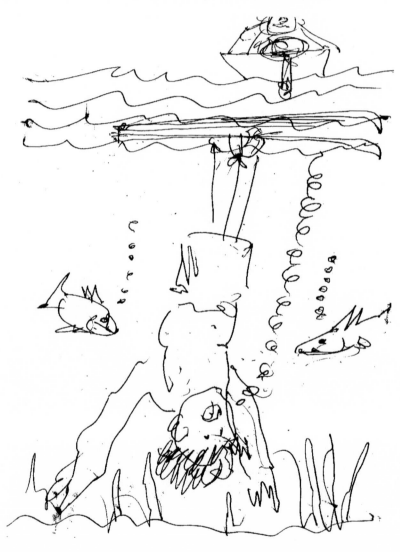

Chapter Twenty-Three
Billy on the Beach

I would never have gone to church except for Ruthie. I was playing keep-away with her younger sister Markee and enjoying the game at that. We were just a gang of teens gathered by the Ellis store on the shores of Sunset Lake. It was mid-summer and I was getting interested in girls as come natural when you reach fifteen. There was a motley crew of us raising a slight amount of Hell and shouting and giggling as teens are want to do of a sunny afternoon.

There was Ronnie LaPrell from the Haverhill pals who stayed at the camp for most of the summer. There was Gayle who was endowed by the Creator with a most pleasant frontal area encased in a loose bathing suit top that woggled most enjoyably when she chased the ball. There was Junior Helkeotis who was calling Halitosis for obvious reasons. Add to that a gaggle of locals of both sexes and you had a really good time.

Mrs. Ellis had tried to shush us a couple of times until her granddaughter Carolyn joined us along with her friend Markee. Then she just shook her grey head and retreated to the comfort of adults in the store. I was taken by Markee's smile and her laugh. So, as luck would have it, I tried to cut her off from the marauding herd to discover more about her. Just as I tossed the ball to her there was a whirl of dust like when the Tasmanian devil enters the scene in a Bugs Bunny cartoon and a vision turned my life upside down. It was Markee's older sister Ruthie and she grabbed the ball in midair and suddenly keep-away turned into try and catch Ruthie.

So, gentle reader, that also became my personal game as well which is why I started going to the Hampstead Congregational Church. Now as you might remember, we hadn't darkened the door or any other part of a church since I was considered unfit for baptism back in an earlier chapter, so the experience was quite new and a bit on the "hocus pocus' side of life for me. But, there I was sitting between Markee and Ruthie in a shirt and tie. They were adorned in starched dresses with petticoats, matching hats and gloves. Most of the people seemed to have been around since God was an altar boy and the pastor person was in a black get-up and seemed like he never smiled. He might have been related to Miss Hoyt. He slicked his black hair straight back and parted it in the middle like a football.

He was really a fun dude when you got him out of that pure white room and upstairs where we had Pilgrim Fellowship. Now think of it a minute. What kind of "fellowship" would you associate with the Pilgrims? Not your most fun crowd, n'est pas?
But, we played games like sardines where you hid in dark places and when others found you they hid there too until the closeness of boys and girls would make a saint blush. I liked that game.

So I was hooked on religion and being close to the female gender in dark (or even light) places. Before long they asked me to join the church and even baptized me with a few sprinkles of water from a magic dish and I was official. After that, they made me the president of the Pilgrim Fellowship, because I was breathing and seemed to attract a lot of kids to the group. That was all well and good until they asked me to give the sermon at Youth Sunday. It was called "the teenagers role in the church" but Miss Bumstead printed it "the teenagers roll in the church" which was probably closer to the truth what with playing "sardines" and all.

They came summer and church camp. We got scholarships and that was cool. The camp was on an island on Lake Whatshmaawhositts or something like that. I signed up Ralph Kelly and of course Markee, Ruthie, and Carolyn Ellis where anxious to attend. Now being on an island we were supposed to pack light, but Ralphie and I were in the middle of our Charles Atlas muscle building binge and we couldn't leave our free weights at home, for crying downtown.

So we loaded them, all 300 pounds plus the bars and collars into Ralphie's Dad old steamer trunk and waited or perhaps "weighted" for the boat to take us to the island camp.

We could pick up the trunk pretty easy but when we swung it over the transom into the boat and two fairly skinny guys grabbed it, they almost went through the floor of the craft into the deep as they called out to the Lord for help. Ralphie looked into the sky and said, "It's my stamp collection. I didn't want my little brother to ruin it." Little did I Know that I was in for a change in all I had planned fro the next fifty years.

The Last Chapter of My First Book
A long and winding road

Some people will tell you that they got a call to serve God. I got more of a nudge to follow Jesus. I was sixteen, living on my own, and ticked off at God (if there was one) for taking my Dad at age 36. We lived in the dying shoe town of Haverhill, Massachusetts. I was the first and only grandchild for 12 years. My favorite adult, Aunt Ethel, had taken me to Catholic Mass several times before God (who seemed to have it in for the Comeau family) took her at age 33.

The dim memories of those services with incense and Latin, were the sum of my exposure to organized religion up to age sixteen. Religion was never discussed in the house. As far as I knew from what I'd overheard, the church was for the poor fools who needed something to hope for after this life, because this life left so much to be desired.

But, I was sixteen and immortal. I was in total control of my destiny. I had left home when my mother started to drink too much after Dad's death. I told her to call me when she got it together and split for New Hampshire. I was boarding with a family, working at the Hampstead Family Market and Gas Station, and had my own car. Sure it was a '41 Ford with no second gear, but it was mine. Then I fell in love, a perplexing malady that strikes all of us from time to time and has a way of changing one's life. I started dating a young woman who went to church every week. So, I went to church every week.

In the front of the Hampstead, NH Congregational Church there was a communion table with the words, "In Remembrance of Me" carved into the wood. I wondered who it was that was so well known that everybody would know who the "Me" was. I figured it was placed there in memory of a former member whom God had "taken" before his or her time. The year that the tight-lipped New Hampshire Congregationalists voted (not unanimously) to join the United Church of Christ, I was baptized by Rev. Ted Hadley and joined the Hampstead Congregational Church. I liked this religion. I still wasn't sure about the God thing, but Jesus was some kind of guy in my book. I also reunited with my mother who had remarried and moved from Haverhill to Hampstead.

That summer I followed my girlfriend to church camp for a week. Now, I was a drummer, so I thought the course called Rhythm Choir was for percussionists. That's how I found myself with 15 girls in a dance choir. I am not a dancer, but I stuck it out. They had me introducing the various dances. One of the girls who were dancing to the Lord's Prayer learned just before the performance that her Dad had died. I could relate. She went on, with tears in her eyes and danced in honor of her Dad. My life changed at that moment. I knew without question that I had to use whatever talents I had to honor my Dad, and if I might be politically incorrect for a moment, the One Jesus called Dad, as well. I guess the power of that dancer's faith had filled my empty soul. It wasn't a call, perhaps, but I felt a definite nudge towards some form of ministry.

When I got back, I told Rev. Hadley that I was going to be a minister. He raised one eyebrow and said something like, " God help the church". As time passed, he accepted the fact that I was serious and talked to me about Bangor Theological Seminary. He had gone there years before, "turning" as he put it, "a fairly talented printer's devil into a moderately passable pulpit jockey." He thought I could get accepted at Bangor, even with my less than sterling grades. In my senior year of High School, I was accepted "In Care" of the Rockingham Association. That fall, after my graduation with a class of 11 seniors from Hampstead High School, I loaded my drum set and all my worldly goods into the 41' Ford and drove due North. And drove, and drove, and drove.

Two things I remember from the first day at BTS. First, we were told that if we really wanted to be a minister, we must be prepared to "pray, preach, or die" at a moment's notice. I was and still am. Secondly, we were asked to look to the right and to the left and realize that one of those we saw would be gone before the year was out. There were three of us, fresh out of high school. I was the only one left after the first semester. After the second semester, I married my High School sweetheart. I was 18. She was 17.

Getting married was her way out of working in a shoe shop, because her Dad didn't believe in "wasting money sending a girl to college". I spent three years at Bangor Seminary: two pre-theological years taking basic college courses plus Coptic Greek, New & Old Testament studies and practical instruction in preaching and leading prayer. I guess they figured that if it came time to die, we'd figure that out on our own. The third year was what most would find in the first year of any seminary. At the end of the third year, I transferred to the University of New Hampshire to finish my BA in History/Education. There were three of us in the Comeau family now.

I was also three years into my ministry. I started in the second semester with a church of my own. The Sandy Point, Maine Congregational Church (no UCC for us, thank you) was tiny, tired, and beautiful beyond belief. I remember two things to this day. One was my organist telling me that my senior deacon, " don't know no more than a dory a-drift." The other memory is of the older woman who told me why she stopped coming to church. "Son, you ain't lived enough, to have sinned enough, to have repented enough, to have anything to preach that I would care to hear!"

I spent the next two years serving as pastor of the Nottingham, New Hampshire Community Church and attending the University of New Hampshire. After graduation I was called to the Danville, New Hampshire Baptist Church where my father had insisted he had met my mother at a dance in the parish hall. My mother claimed that since the Baptist's didn't dance, it was probably the Grange hall.

I spent a year as the pastor of this church and the teaching-principal of the Nottingham Elementary school. I was also Dean of Senior High Fellowship Camps for the New Hampshire Conference of the UCC, a position I held for three years. After a year in Danville, I received a call to be Minister of Education at the First Church of Christ, Congregational in Keene, NH. I loved that church at the head of the square, at the end of America's widest Main Street.

It was in the park across the street from the church that I finally learned the secret of New Hampshire (read Swamp Yankee) humor. One day, Uncle Fred, a senior deacon, was waiting in the fall sunshine for a meeting to start 'cross the street. I walked over and noticed him trying to light his ever-present pipe with a wooden match. Unfortunately, he was using the wrong end of the match. I pointed out the folly of his action. "Uncle Fred", says I, " I think you're trying to light the wrong end of that match." Without missing a beat he replied. "Heck, boy…any damn fool can light the other end."

In Keene, I worked on my Master's degree in Education at Keene State College. After two years, I decided to attempt to finish my seminary work. I was called to become the Minister of Youth at the New Britain, Connecticut United Church of Christ, just 10 miles from the Hartford Seminary Foundation. I was accepted as a second semester junior, based on my BTS work. Over the next three years, I took courses and built a large youth program, including starting and managing two coffeehouse ministries. One called the Inn, was located downtown in the basement of South Church, oriented towards young adults and folk music. The second, The Galloping Elephant, was on the campus of the local teacher's college and served as a base for the campus ministry.

I also helped form, the Incredible Broadside Brass Bed Band. This musical group would entertain at coffeehouses, college concerts and continue for the next twenty years. This group also released several singles and albums of satire and message songs that gained national airplay. The last semester of my senior year, I applied for an independent study program. My proposal was that I write and produce a series of films, poetry books, music and spoken word albums, and teaching guides to help make the Gospel more understandable to the 60's youth culture.

I was also called by the First Congregational Church of Old Greenwich, Connecticut to become their first Minister of Youth & Education. There were now four children in the Comeau household. In Old Greenwich, I helped build youth fellowships that grew to over 100 young people from the church and the community. The program included: the Saturday Cinematographers; a coffee house; an art and discussion gallery; a summer program of Religion and the Arts, a drama group, a weekly radio ministry; and a youth edited poetry and religion column in the local paper.

It was here also that my life imploded and my career exploded. Before I could present my "independent study" to the Hartford professors (the materials that were all completed, published and nationally distributed. Also, my Mom died, my marriage failed, and I entered a deep depression that kept me in the valley of darkness for two years. I supported myself with my music, sleeping in a 1962 Chevy convertible that was given to me by a friend from Old Greenwich.

I followed the same path of drinking too much that had captured my Mom years before. I was 30 and I felt my life was over. Then I met a Methodist minister who gave me a shot at running his church coffeehouse. That grew into a job as his associate minister and I was back. The Broadside Brass Bed Band had a couple of hits. I was running a multi-faceted youth program, and on the road to recovery. Since I was working in a Methodist Church, I followed the Methodist plan for ordination. After examining my credentials, my education was rounded out with three classes at Union Theological Seminary, seminars in Methodist polity, and psychological testing at a denominationally approved clinic.

In June 1972, I was ordained a Deacon in the United Methodist Church. I was assigned to a small parish in Stamford, Connecticut and finished my year of practical service needed to be ordained as an Elder. During that year, however, to supplement my income I also worked on Madison Avenue as a junior copywriter. That experience lead me to ask for a leave of absence from the ministry to follow a career in the advertising profession. That "leave" has lasted too many years. I feel like I spent most of that time trying to light the wrong end of a match. I made money and I won many awards, but something important was missing.

During this time, however, I never gave up my desire to use my talents to honor my Dad, the teachings of Jesus, or the sharing of the Good News of God's unconditional love. I served as a fill-in minister for friends, taught Sunday school and served as deacon at many churches, and participated in fund-raiser events for local churches and several UCC conferences. I created and had published several scripture based poetry books (United Church Press and the Upper Room Press). I authored, produced and directed five plays for young people (published by Baker's Plays and Contemporary Drama Service).

I wrote, produced and directed 24 children's audio products-two of which were Grammy finalists (released by Avant Garde Records, Sine Qua Non Records, and North Star Records) and 12 children's video products (Advanced Video Group & Best Video) that won the Parent's Choice Award. All my work is based on teaching the principles of Christian living in a way that is understandable to young people.

I also helped my son take a concept called JCGear from a small local positive message apparel store on the beach in Fort

Lauderdale to become a publicly trading company offering child-safe internet services and family-values products. This has allowed me to get back in the recording studio to re-master many of my early works and create new audio products. My latest release featuring the voices and musical talents of two of my five children, is a CD of scripture, poetry and songs honoring the martyrs and survivors of Columbine High School in Colorado.

When I finally remarried in 1981, I was Senior Vice President and Creative Director of Creamer Advertising with offices in Providence, New York, Hartford, and Pittsburgh.

Five years later, my wife and I welcomed our first (my fifth) child and joined the Woodridge United Church of Christ. I have served on almost every committee, as a deacon and now as member at large. Over the years, I have tried to serve as a confidant to the ministers, having been there, done that. I have worked with the Conference to develop the radio ministry, fundraising video programs and materials for Synod 22.

Now, I have lived enough, to have sinned enough, to have repented enough to have something to say that I hope is worth hearing. So, I returned to the ministry on a part-time basis as pastor of the United Church of Assonet, Massachusetts, member of United Church of Christ. Now into my tenth year, as using my newly minted PhD in the Creative Arts from Evangelical Theological Seminary, I have begun teaching college courses in Coping with Life, Death, and Dying. The chapter of this book by the same name gave birth to the notion to remember the early stuff. That's how this book came to be, and I really hope you enjoy it.

Bill Comeau
Winter 2009-2010

Later Reflections:

Adam's last son

Naked as a Jaybird
Arrows long and tooth-like
Bow shaped with monkey jaw file
Listens to the chatter of dinner
In the rich canopy above

Death released
Body falls to feed his family,
When the white devils grab him
Drag him to the waiting floating dungeon
Spoon-like chained to strangers,
Sleeping in own filth.

Cargo waxed with chicken grease
On the auction block
Naked as a jaybird
Good strong black buck
Brings strong dollars for Cotton Kings

And proper New England merchants
Who own the churches

Where the pure white pastors
Preach about a pure white heaven and our pure WHITE GOD
But when the modern day preacher
Who is more of a prophet
Rattles our Red White and Blue world
Asking his God to damn it all,
America that is,

We shudder as the tooth-like truth
Stabs our monkey skin
Brings us crashing down to earth.

Down to earth.
"Ashes to Ashes
All fall down."

Mister Saigon

*Reflections on the presentation of "Miss Saigon" at the
Providence Performing Arts Center, January 12, 2003*

Back stage the stagehands get ready with their biggest trick. It
always gets the biggest audience reaction.
Forget about the tall handsome actor with the powerful voice,
The oriental actress that has simply nailed the lead role.
Great extras. I loved the Engineer…

The Engineer knew how to "get things to happen"
Not always on the right side of the law.
I knew the Engineer.

I worked with him in a band once.
He had stolen 31 cars while still in High School.
Just stole cars with the keys in the ignition.
Drove 'em 'till they ran out of gas and walked away.

He lived on the ragged edge of polite society and early death.
Billy engineered until his inheritance ran out and his girl ran out and
his friend Boozer gave him a transfer over the line.
Dust in the wind. His lonely stone reads "Peace at Last".

Billy would have been great back stage.
Could have been a Best Boy.

He could rig a car with a paperclip and a rubber band.
So, he'd be a natural back stage.
He would have smiled as the life-sized replica chopper
Materialized above the frightened actors heads
Props whirring
Noise deafening

Audience gasping at the reality of it all
As America symbolically left Viet Nam
As the dust of the world stirred in the streets

As Miss Saigon became a dream name shouted in a midwestern bedroom

Wife wondering about her husband.
Husband never able to leave Nam completely
Nobody ever left Nam completely.
Art and Rich and Joe and Pete and Captain Dave

And so many others.
All those names on a black shiny wall.
All those faces on the evening news.
Death brought into our living rooms by Walter Cronkite and Texaco.

Memories of Viet Nam.
Then there was…my oldest "son". His name is Ronny.
He became my oldest "son" for a few years in the mid-60's.
I was the young minister who got along with kids.
I played guitar
Love Rock 'n Roll

Formed a band with the town least likely kids and gave 'em instruments and Matching shirts and Pride and Dreams and Confidence.

Ronny was Mr. Keyboards for the Crescendos.
He lived on the edge.Engineer boots, Faded Jeans, White T-shirt with a pack of Marlboros rolled up in the right sleeve…
Leather Jacket, black hair slicked back.

Held with spit and more than a dab of BrylCream
Ronny had Elvis hair… Buddy Holly glasses
And an Olympic class smile.
And the girls…. well I mean.

That's why when I moved my family to Keene New Hampshire.
Ronny came with us.
His folks asked if he could go with…
"The only one he seems to listen to"
So at the tender age of 25 I inherited

A sixteen year old Rock /n Roll keyboard player son.

It worked out fine.We had two little kids, my wife's 15-year-old brother living with us to escape his abusive father and...A sixteen-year-old Rock and Roll keyboard player.
Ronny stayed with us until he graduated High School...
Squeaked through High School but graduated.

In the same class with Martha who would become Mrs.Ronnie, when he came home on an extended leave from the Marines, just before he shipped off to Nam.

He had two sets of proud parents that day.

I got letters; Martha got letters, his folks in Danville got letters.
In their letters he was doing fine.
In mine he told the truth.
He was having a tough time.
He wondered about those he fixed in his sites.
They were the enemy and they needed to die.
They needed to die because...
Because, because, because...because of the wonderful life there was...Waiting back in Keene with Martha and his band buddies and his two families... and maybe someday...his own family.

He began visiting a local orphanage in his free time
He played music for the kids.
He sang to them and they clapped along.
Two languages, one song.
I'd like to teach the world to sing.
But the harmony turned sour when "the enemy"
Took all the kids from the orphanage as a human shield.

There was one little girl who reminded him of Martha.
Olympic class smile in spite of it all.

He had written to Martha about her. He wanted to see
If they could adopt her after the conflict was over...but it never was really over. It still isn't to this day.
He had asked me to look into the paperwork stateside.

It wasn't going to be easy.

Then there came the day he went to visit and they were all gone.

He volunteered to go on the search and rescue mission.
In his letter to me he told me about tracking them to a lonely mountain pass, where the "enemy" no longer needed human hostages.

He said he sat holding the one who might have been his daughter one day and in that time the war became very personal.

It was no longer someone else's war.
It had nothing to do with Capitalism verses Communism.
It wasn't about crossing imaginary geographic lines.
They had invaded his imaginary stateside backyard and stolen his child and murdered her…with all her friends…and teachers.
Dust of the world swept away.
Collateral damage.

From that day to this, a part of Mr. Keyboards is forever cradling what might have been in his strong arms and hating with every fiber of his being, a world let lets children become…expendable.

When I think of Ronny, I always go back to Keene and the summer before he left.
We are sitting under parachutes around tables that were recently giant spools for telephone wire. The coffee house was called the Fish.
There is a red-checkered tablecloth with wax spills decorating the center. There are red glass candleholders with what looks like string inside them. It is imperative that any young man sitting at the table must light the candle and let the melted wax cover his fingers. That's what Charlie was doing.

Ronny is playing the piano and Martha is hanging over the edge totally transfixed with that kind of young love that catches up with all of us at 18.

I am sitting at the table with kids from the youth group and a young Episcopal Seminarian who will be leaving next week to become a civil rights worker in the South.

Ronny and Martha joined us as I opened the pizza box and the young seminarian; Jonathan Daniels pours orange soda into paper cups.

We stop for a minute. Silence. It happens every so often. One of the kids...Charlie... stops with pizza inches from his open mouth and says, "What?"
"Is this the way the disciples felt in that upper room?" Ron asks me. "I'm sure it was," Jonathan replies. "We got better stuff to eat," quipped Charlie digging into crust, cheese and sauce with the ferocity only a hungry teen can deliver. "They had better stuff to drink"; Martha added sipping the orange soda (called "tonic" in New Hampshire).

I remember that as clear as if it were two weeks ago. Partially because two weeks ago on a Wednesday morning as I was unlocking my office and the phone was ringing. Out of the blue, it was Charlie. He found me on-line at our website. He wanted to say thanks for things I had forgotten. The coffee house had made a difference in his life.

In September, Ron Brown went to war and came back, like all the veterans did, with first-hand knowledge of how a war can start as a job to do and become something more than you could have ever imagined, and would never forget.

Jonathan Daniels went south determined to show God's love for all God's children. He did just that when he stepped between an angry man's shotgun and the black girl he was walking with. She lived. Jonathan didn't.

And I stayed in Keene for a while before moving to Hartford to complete my seminary education. I watched the protestors standing in the middle of the Square wanting the war over, now! I attended the memorial service at the Episcopal Church. I talked for hours with the kids in the coffee house who wanted to protest the war, to move to Canada, to enlist as soon as they turned eighteen, to start a new country on an island...

So, when the chopper imagery filled the stage at the PPAC, last Sunday afternoon, I was no longer in Providence. I was reliving Ron's letter's and Captain Dave's stories and Joe's experience in a Hooch with a reel to reel tape deck and some great tunes. I was sitting with Pete Levin in the back of the van after we had played another gig in Buffalo and listening to the stories of those he played with in Nam, young musicians who never returned.

And so today as they march again in the streets protesting a war that does not yet exist, but is but a heartbeat away...I stand again watching from a distance.

I want the war go away, or rather...never start.
War only gives us rain in graveyards with gunshots and lonely bugle songs and flags folded exactly, precisely...and put into the arms of loved ones who would trade all the flags ever made for one more hug from their dear dear son or daughter.

War rearranges boundary lines for those who are fools enough to think any piece of God's green earth can actually belong to anyone.

A few more turns of this molten ball and ice descends to claim deeded rights for the next million years.

We live for moments, yet we try to control the who and what and where of this life as if we would be here for eons.

God forgive our shallow view.

So I stand watching, praying that we will not again send young men and women into harm's way.

But, I have watched for a long time now. Uncle Joe and Al came home from battle and never talked about what they faced in the South Pacific.

I listened to teachers who were protecting parallels in Korea, the last time around.

I remember stories for Captain Dave who dedicated his first years back sponsoring and settling immigrants from Southeast Asia in Rhode Island. I gave Ron back his letters. Pete and I still touch base.

I listened to the Dad's whose sons were in harm's way the last time Battle Storms shed blood and innocence on desert sands.

And I pray for peace but I must stand with those who are our brave protectors and put their lives between those who would destroy in the name of their God.

I need to be with those who from this church and this town and this state and these United States: who step to the line, ready to offer their last full measure of devotion to protect those they love more than life itself.

If I thought marching in a protest would end or prevent a war and not be seen as a lack of support for those who lives are on the line. Well, who wouldn't stand tall for peace? If we were to vote for or against war, mark me as against.

But first, count me as supporting our brothers and sisters who have sworn to protect us. Those who have taken the oath to go into burning buildings and keep our streets and neighborhoods safe, and be deployed to hostile environments to draw lines in the sand.

I say, "God Bless you all for what you have done and will do."
And, we will support you and work with every fiber of our being to help create a world that is more understanding and forgiving and does not look at the differences but celebrates the similarities that one day

All God's Children might know peace on earth.
Amen

Abandoned and Blue

It was a cold day in February (is there any other kind) and I had just finished a painting called Abandoned and Blue. It was hanging at the Providence Art Club. Needless to say I was feeling sorry for myself. Oh, come on, you feel that way too sometimes, 'fess up. So my cure for the winter blues was to head for my favorite breakfast place. As soon as I got through the door I could see I was in the right place. Also I could see that I wasn't the only one who uses breakfast as therapy for a chilly mood.

The place was alive with happy chatter. The hostess greeted me by name (Think Cheers with eggs). Before I could bring myself back down with "Party of One, please", her smile brought back the sunshine. I settled in and waved to a few friends.

Then came the next problem, which was what to have. The hot coffee was on the table before I got through page one of the menu. So, which of my favorites would it be? I remember the morning I was sharing breakfast with Max Mays, the Rhode Island Treasure and he named Tony's waffle covered with the dazzling colors of fresh fruit "The Rose Window". It does have spiritual healing power for a day like today.

Then there's the hash, O My Goodness, there's nothing like home-made hash to make eggs know their purpose in life. If you're Anthony you splash 'em with hot sauce (makes your eyes light up and your tummy say Howdy). I prefer them over easy and on top of the hash. A little pepper and I'm in Heaven's waiting room.

But wait…there's more, as my pals the Ginsu Boys used to say. One of my personal delights is two poached eggs sitting on grilled English muffins with bacon and home fries. If your parents didn't scare all the fun out of you when you were a kid, you can arrange the bacon into eyebrows and a 'stash and have breakfast with Grouch Marx.

By now I am in a giddy mood and my waitperson (to be politically correct) has refilled my coffee with a smile and told me about the specials. "Oh Yummy", I utter and order something entirely different. What did I get gentle reader? A heapin' helpin' of wholesome comfort on a chilly winter's morning.

Memo to Mel:

Mel, Bubalah! Rumor has it you're about to redo the Christ thing again. Been done.
To Death!
Nobody Cares.
Also hear by the poolside that you're going OUTSIDE the CLUB.
Naughty. Naughty.
You'll never make a dime.
Nobody. And I mean NOBODY will pick it up, distribution-wise.

Let's look at the project from a dollar and cents, make that sense prospective.

The plot is old hat:
Poor Jewish kid makes good. Society nails him. He wins with some slight of soul illusion. Maybe Babs will write a song. Wind, wings, all that jazz.

And, not for not…but who are you bad guys.
Don't blame the Jews, for the love of God.

Totally politically incorrect in this town.
You'll never work here again, kid.

And, the Romans, well they are now the Family and that's not wise-guy, if "youse get my drift."
If there's anyway you can dump the blame on Bin Laden or his great Grand Pappy, maybe you got something. But probably not.

I've had research done and there's this part of the story where this Jesus kid says," So, do you think I could not appeal to my Father and he would send legions of angels to destroy all my enemies…"
Now, something like that. Talk about an ending.

Anyway, if you're still gonna do it don't say I didn't warn ya."

Your agent,
Balls McCarthy

Stay Tuned for further adventures from Bangor Seminary to Madison Avenue in my next book: "You've Got to be Kidding."